FLOWER POWER

FOR UKULELE

Arranged by Nancy Piver

T0039734

ISBN 978-1-4234-9854-4

HAL•LEONARD®
CORPORATION
7777 W. BLUEMOUND RD. P.O. BOX 13819 MILWAUKEE, WI 53213

Visit Hal Leonard Online at
www.halleonard.com

CONTENTS

Abraham, Martin and John

Words and Music by Richard Holler

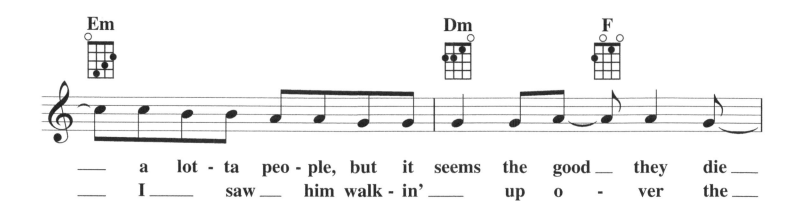

— a lot-ta peo-ple, but it seems the good ___ they die ___
— I ___ saw ___ him walk-in' ___ up o - ver the ___

___ young. You know I just looked a - round ___ and he's
___ hill. with A - bra-ham, Mar - tin, ___ and ___

| 1., 2. | | 3., 4. | *Fine* |

gone. _____
gone. _____
John. _____

Bridge

Did-n't you love _____ the things ___ that they ___

6

___ stood   for? _   Did-n't they   try _____

to find   some   good _____   for   you and   me?

And   we'll _____ be   free.   Some -

D.C. al Fine

day   soon _____   it's   gon - na   be ___   one   day.

(It's A) Beautiful Morning

Words and Music by Felix Cavaliere and Edward Brigati, Jr.

Dm

Gm7

_3_

weath - er's fine and you've got the time. _____
cov - er ground you could-n't _____ keep me down. _____

Am

Dm

It's your chance to wake up and plan __ an - oth - er
It just ain't no good if the sun __ shines and you're

1.

Gm7

C7sus4

C6

2.

Gm7

brand new day.(Ei-ther way.) 2. It's a beau-ti-ful still in- side, (shoot-ing high.)

C7sus4

C7

Still in - side, (shoot-ing high.) _ Still in-side, (shoot-ing high.) Oh, oh. _____

Interlude

F

Am

9

Bridge

There will be chil - dren with rob - ins and flow - ers.

Sun - shine ca - ress - es each new wak - ing ho - ur.

Seems to me that peo - ple keep see - ing more and

more to - day. (Got - ta say.) Lead the way. (It's o - kay.) _

C7sus4

Brand new day. (Got - ta say.) It's o - kay. (All the way.)

More to - day. (Got - ta say.) (Lead the way.) Oh._____

Outro

F   Am

Gm7   C7sus4   C7

N.C.   F

Oh,   oh._____

Blowin' in the Wind

Words and Music by Bob Dylan

F	C		G7					
sleeps	in the	sand? ___				Yes, and	how ___
lowed	to be	free? ___				Yes, and	how ___
hear	peo - ple	cry? ____				Yes, and	how ___

C				F		
___	man - y	times ___		must	the	can -
___	man - y	times ___		can	a	man ___
___	man - y	deaths ___		will	it	take ___

G			C		
non	- balls ___	fly ____	be - fore ___	they are	for -
___	turn his	head ___	and pre - tend	that he just ___
___	'til he	knows ___	that ___ too	man - y	peo -

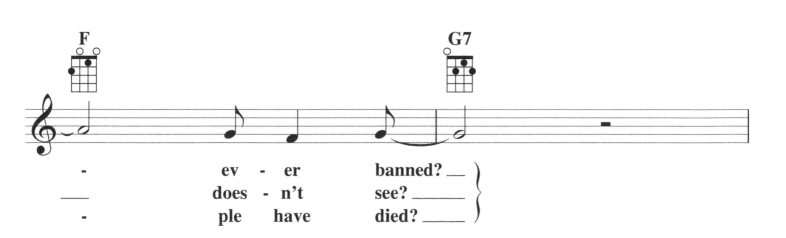

F			G7	
-	ev - er	banned? ___	
___	does - n't	see? _____	
-	ple have	died? _____	

13

California Dreamin'

Words and Music by John Phillips and Michelle Phillips

First note

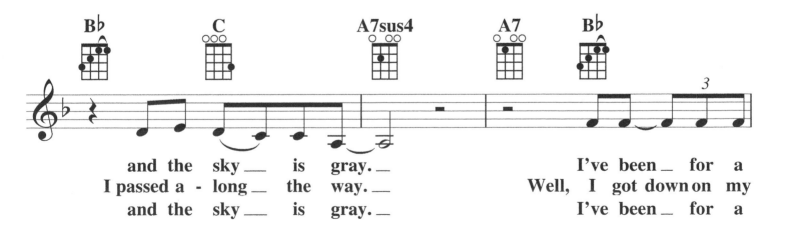

walk   on a win-ter's day. ___
knees   and I pre-tend to pray. ___
walk   on a win-ter's day. ___

I'd be safe and warm, ___
You know the preach-er, like the cold, ___
If I did-n't tell her,

if I was in L. A. ___
he knows I'm gon - na stay. ___
I could leave to - day. ___

Cal - i - for - nia

To Coda ⊕

1.

dream-in'   on such a win-ter's day. ___   2. Stopped in - to a

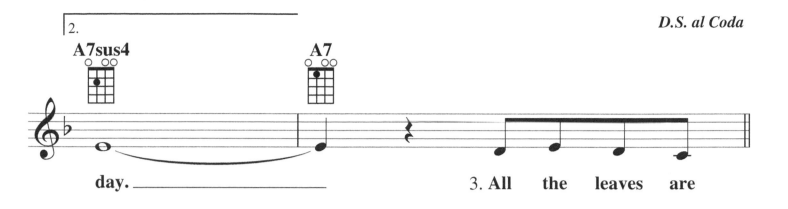

2.

A7sus4   A7

day. _____   3. All   the   leaves   are

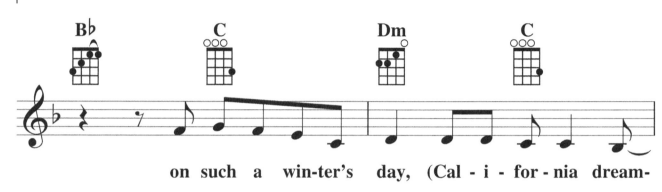

Coda

Bb   C   Dm   C

on   such   a   win-ter's   day,   (Cal - i - for - nia   dream-

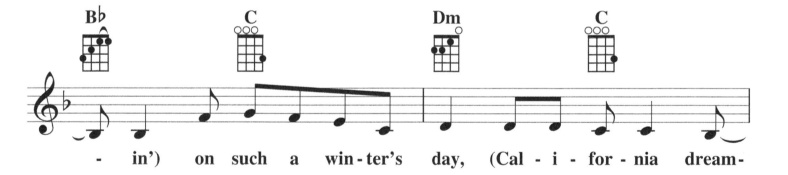

Bb   C   Dm   C

- in')   on   such   a   win - ter's   day,   (Cal - i - for - nia   dream-

Bb   C   Bbmaj7   Dm

- in')   on   such   a   win-ter's   day. _____

Daydream

Words and Music by John Sebastian

1. What a day for a day - dream, ___
2. I've been hav - ing a sweet ___ dream, ___
3. *Whistle*

what a day for a day-dream-in' boy. _____
I've been dream - in' since I woke up to - day. _____

And I'm lost in a day - dream, _____
It's star - ring me in my sweet ___ dream, _____

dream - in' 'bout my bun - dle of joy. _____
'cause she's the one makes me feel ___ this way. ___

And   e - ven   if   time   ain't   real - ly
And   e - ven   if   time   is   pass - ing me
(3.) And   you   can   be   sure   that   if   you're

on my   side, __   it's one of those days for tak - ing a
by a   lot, __   I could - n't care less a - bout __ the
feel - in' right, __   a day-dream will last a - long __

walk   out -   side. _____
dues   you   say   I _____   got.
in - to   the   night. _____

I'm   blow - ing   the   day   to   take   a
To - mor - row   I'll   pay   the   dues   for
To - mor - row   at   break - fast   you   may

- dream, _ cus - tom made for a day - dream - in' boy. _

And I'm lost in a day - dream, _____

dream - in' 'bout my bun - dle of joy. ___

Outro

Whistle

Repeat & fade

21

Daydream Believer

Words and Music by John Stewart

2.

C	Am	Dm7	G7	C

shav-ing raz-or's   cold __ and it   stings. _____

𝄋 **Chorus**

F	G7	Em	F	G7

Cheer up, sleep - y   Jean. _____   Oh, what can it

Am	F	C	F

mean   to   a   day - dream be - liev - er   and   a

To Coda ⊕

C	Am	D7	G7

home - com-ing   queen. _____

Verse

C	Dm	Em

3. You once thought of   me   as   a   white knight on   his
(4.) good times start and   end   with-out   dol - lar one to

steed.
spend. But

Now you know how hap-py I can

be. _____ 4. Oh, and our how much, ba-by,

D.S. al Coda

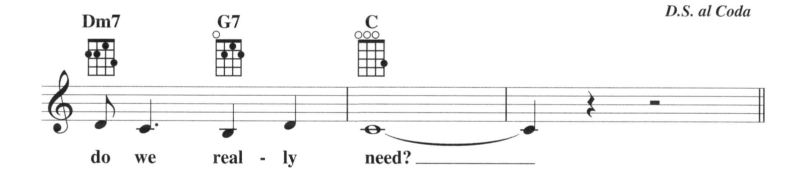

do we real - ly need? _____

⊕ **Coda**

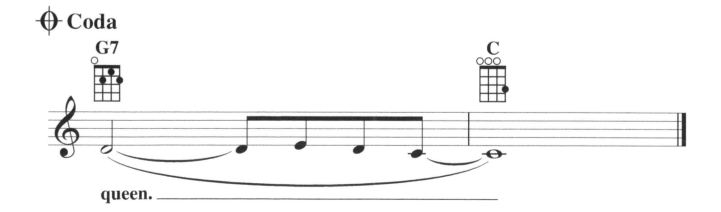

queen. _____

Everybody's Talkin'
(Echoes)

from MIDNIGHT COWBOY
Words and Music by Fred Neil

1., 4. Ev-'ry-bod-y's   talk - in' at me.   I don't hear a

word they're say   -   in',   on -ly the ech-oes ____ of my

mind. _____

2. **Peo - ple**
3. *Instrumental*

stop-pin', star - in'.   I   can't   see   the   fac - es,

on - ly   the   shad - ows _____   of   their   eyes. _____

Chorus

____   I'm   go - in' where the   sun __   keeps shin - in'

through the pour-in'   rain.   Go - in' where the

26

weath - er ___ suits my clothes. _____ Bank - in' off of the

north-east wind. Sail - in' on sum-mer breeze.

Skip-pin' o - ver the o - cean like a stone. _____

2nd time, D.S. al Coda   Coda   Outro

_____   _____ And I won't let you

Repeat & fade

leave my love _ be - hind. _____   And

The 59th Street Bridge Song
(Feelin' Groovy)

Words and Music by Paul Simon

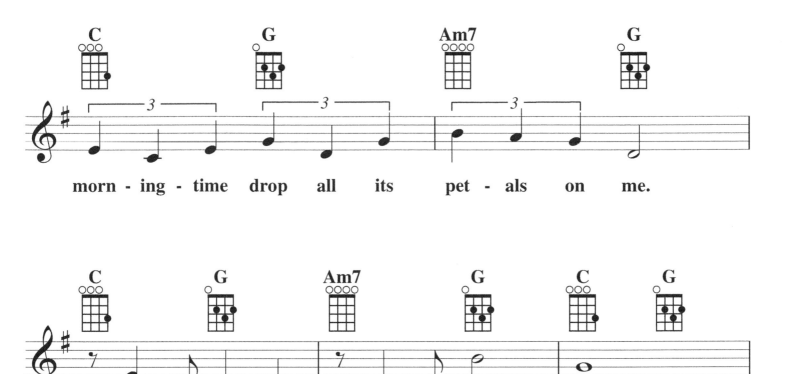

morn - ing - time drop all its pet - als on me.

Life, I love you. All is groov - y.

Outro

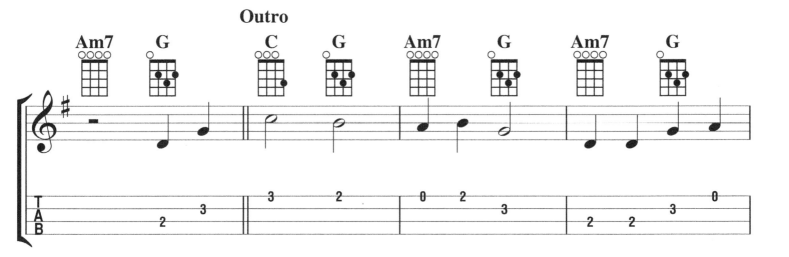

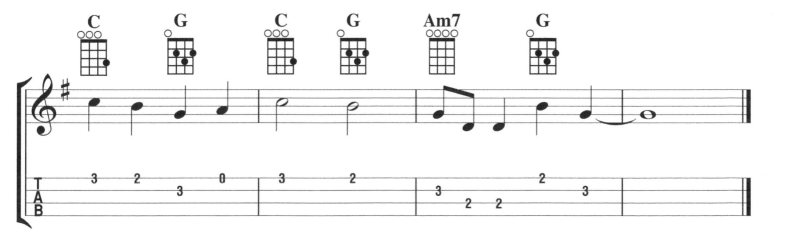

Get Together

Words and Music by Chet Powers

1. Love is but a song we sing. ____ Fear's the way we
2. Some may come and some may go. ____ He will sure-ly
3. If you hear the song I sing, ____ you will un-der-

die. ____ You can make the ____
pass. ____ When the one that ____
stand. ____ *Spoken: Listen.* You hold the key to _____

____ moun-tains ring or make the an - gels
____ left us here re - turns for us at
____ love and fear, all in your trem - bling

cry. ___
last. ___
hand. ___

Know the bird ___ is
We are but ___ a
Just one key ___ un -

on the wing, ___
mo-ment's sun-light
locks them both; ___

and you may not know why. ___
fad-ing in the grass. ___
it's there at your com - mand. ___

Chorus

Come on ___ peo - ple, now, smile on your broth - er. Ev-'ry-bod -

To Coda ⊕

- y get to-geth-er, try to love one an-oth-er right now.

1.

2.

Come on ___ peo - ple, now,   smile on your broth - er. Ev - 'ry-bod -

- y get to - geth - er, try to love one an - oth - er right now.

⊕ Coda

D.C. al Coda
(take repeat)

F

Come on ___ peo - ple, now,

smile on your broth - er. Ev - 'ry-bod - y get to-geth - er, try to

love one an - oth - er right now. Right now! Right now! ___

Groovin'

Words and Music by Felix Cavaliere and Edward Brigati, Jr.

First note

Verse
Moderately slow

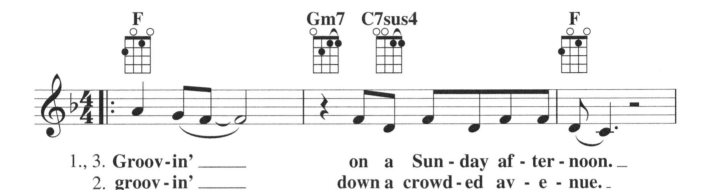

1., 3. Groov-in' _____ on a Sun-day af-ter-noon. _
2. groov-in' _____ down a crowd-ed av-e-nue. _

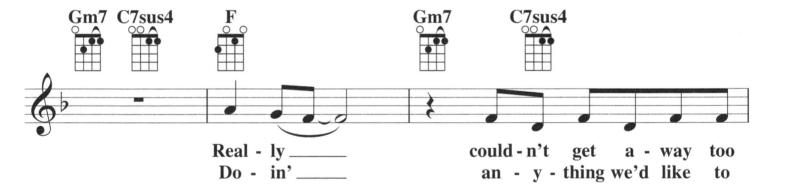

Real-ly _____ could-n't get a-way too
Do-in' _____ an-y-thing we'd like to

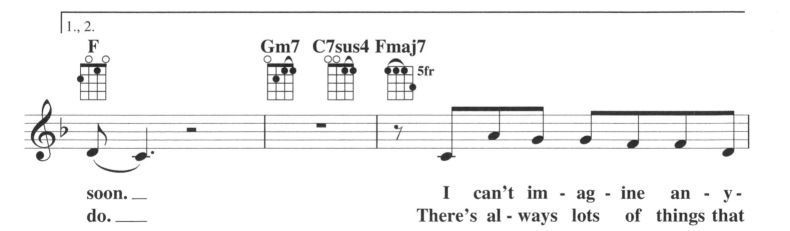

1., 2.

soon. _ I can't im-ag-ine an-y-
do. _ There's al-ways lots of things that

Fmaj7   Gm7

I feel it com - in' clos - er day by day. _____

Bb   Am   Gm7   C6

Life would be ec - sta - sy. You and me end - less - ly

F   Gm7   C7sus4   F

groov - in' _____ on a Sun-day af - ter - noon. _

Gm7   C7sus4   F   Gm7   C7sus4

Real - ly _____ could-n't get a - way too

F   Gm7   C7sus4   F

soon, no, no, no, no. Groov - in'. _____

Happy Together

Words and Music by Garry Bonner and Alan Gordon

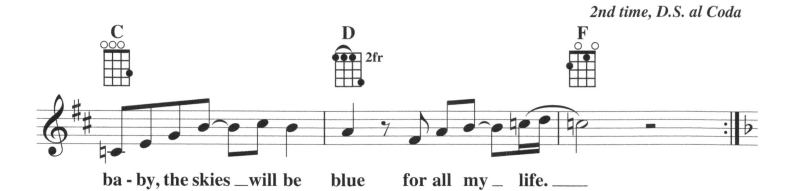

ba - by, the skies __will be   blue   for all my _ life. ____

Coda

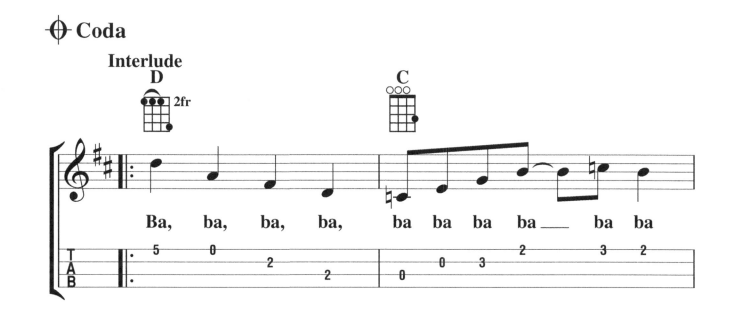

Interlude

Ba,   ba,   ba,   ba,   ba ba ba ba ____ ba ba

ba,   ba ba ba   ba.

Verse

5. Me and you   and you and me.   No mat-ter how they tossed the dice,   it had to

He Ain't Heavy, He's My Brother

Words and Music by Bob Russell and Bobby Scott

First note

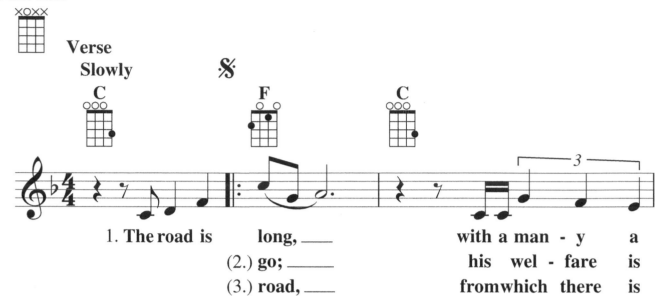

1. The road is   long, ___   with a man - y   a
(2.) go; ___   his wel - fare   is
(3.) road, ___   from which there   is

wind - ing ___ turn, _____   that leads ___ us to   who   knows
my   con - cern. _____   No bur - den is   he   to
no   re - turn. _____   While we're ___ on the   way   to

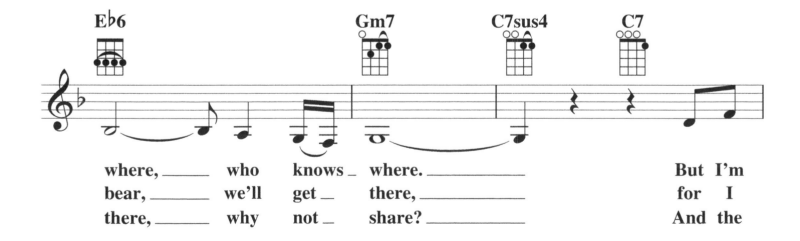

where, _____   who   knows _ where. _____   But I'm
bear, _____   we'll   get _   there, _____   for I
there, _____   why   not _   share? _____   And the

strong, _____
know _____
load _____

strong e-nough to car - ry
he would not en-cum - ber
does-n't weigh me down __ at

To Coda ⊕

him;
me;
all;

he ain't __ heav-y, _____

he's my broth-er. _____

1.

2. So on we

2.

If I'm

Bridge

lad-en at all, _____

I'm lad-en with

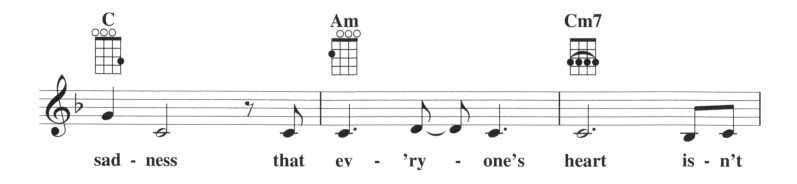

sad - ness　　　that　ev - 'ry - one's　heart　is - n't

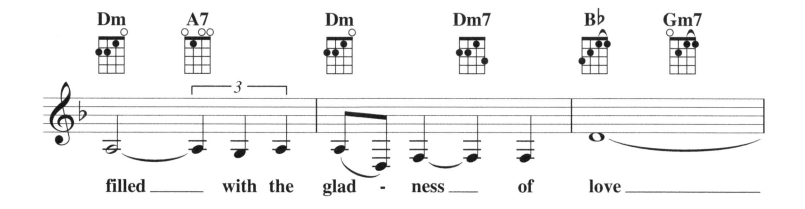

filled _____ with the glad - ness _____ of love _____

D.S. al Coda

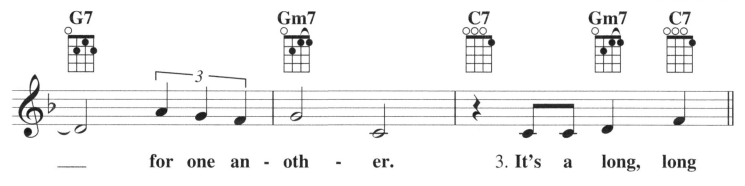

_____ for one an - oth - er.　3. It's a long, long

🎵 **Coda**

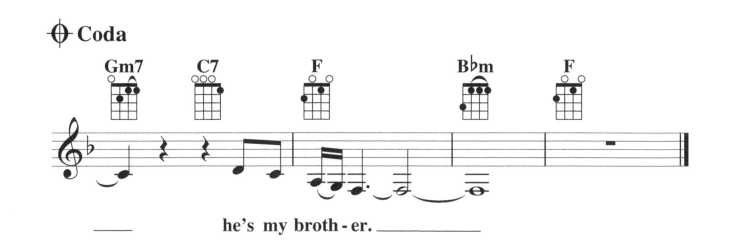

_____ he's my broth - er. _____

It Never Rains in Southern California

Words and Music by Albert Hammond and Michael Hazlewood

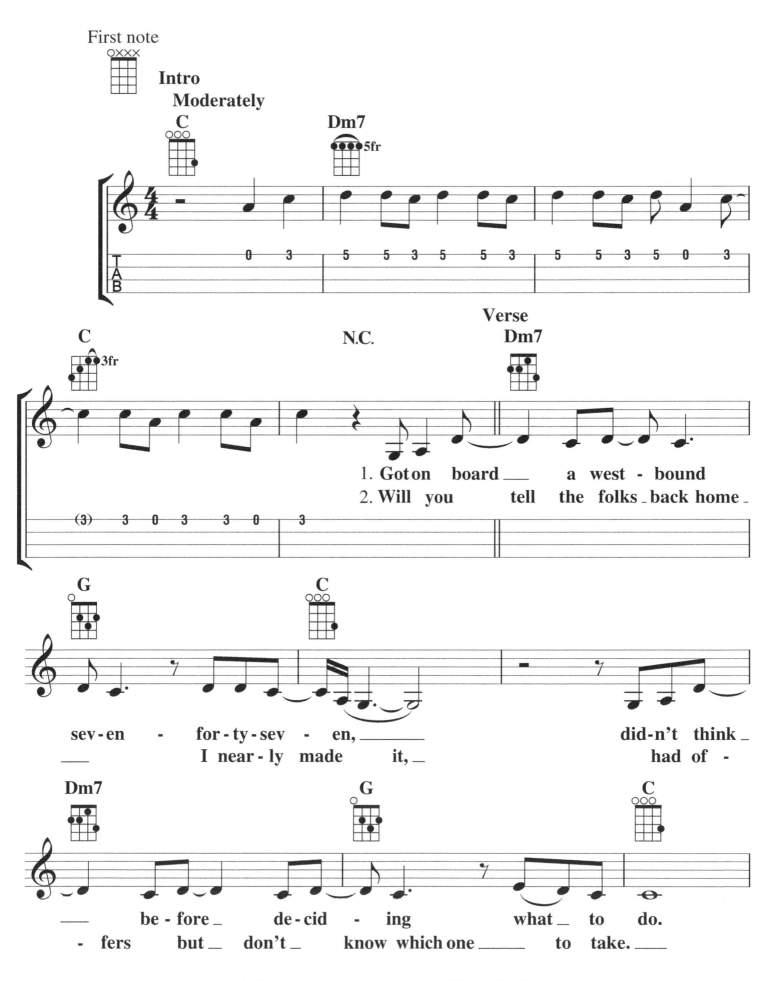

of talk ___ be - fore. ___ It nev - er

rains in Cal - i - for - nia, ___ but

girl, don't they warn ___ ya, ___ it pours ___

To Coda ⊕

___ man, ___ it pours. ___ Out of

Bridge

work, I'm out - ta my head, ___ out of self re -

spect, I'm out - ta bread. _____ I'm un - der -

loved, I'm un - der - fed. _____ I wan - na go

home. It nev - er rains in Cal - i - for -

- nia, _____ but girl, don't they warn

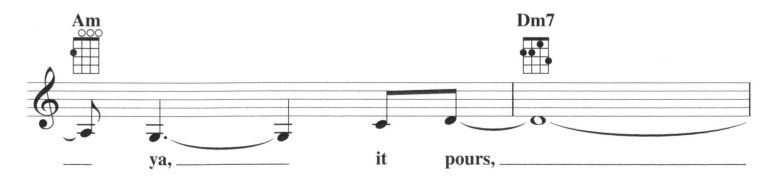

_____ ya, _____ it pours, _____

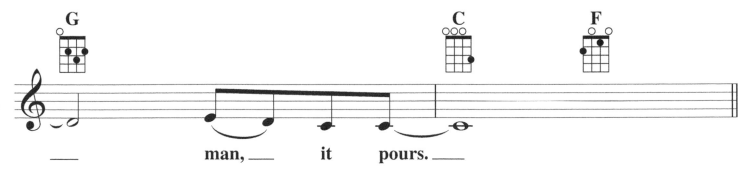

man, ___ it pours. ___

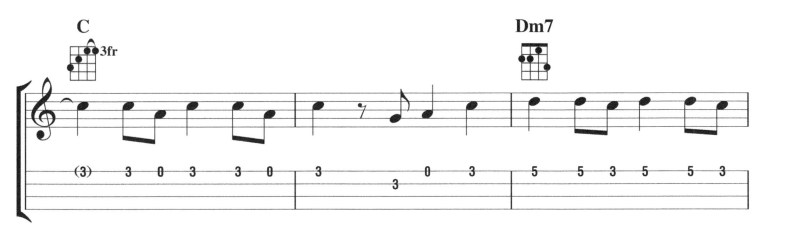

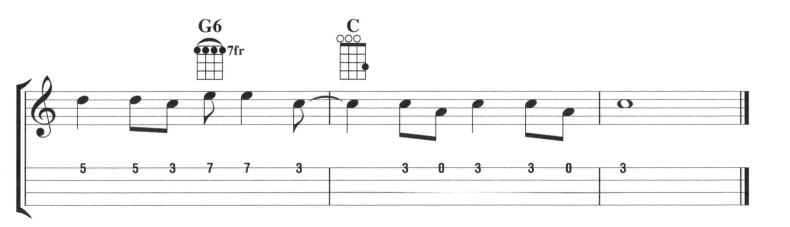

Joy to the World

Words and Music by Hoyt Axton

First note

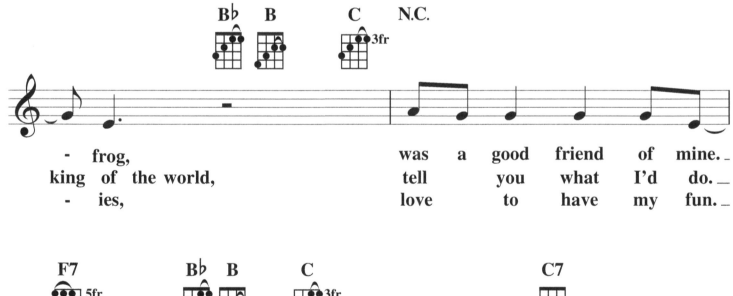

1. Jer - e - mi - ah was a bull -
2. If I were __ the
3. Y'know I love the lad -

- frog,   was a good friend of mine. __
king of the world,   tell you what I'd do. __
- ies,   love to have my fun. __

I nev - er un - der - stood a sin - gle
I'd throw a - way the cars and the
I'm a high night fly - er and a

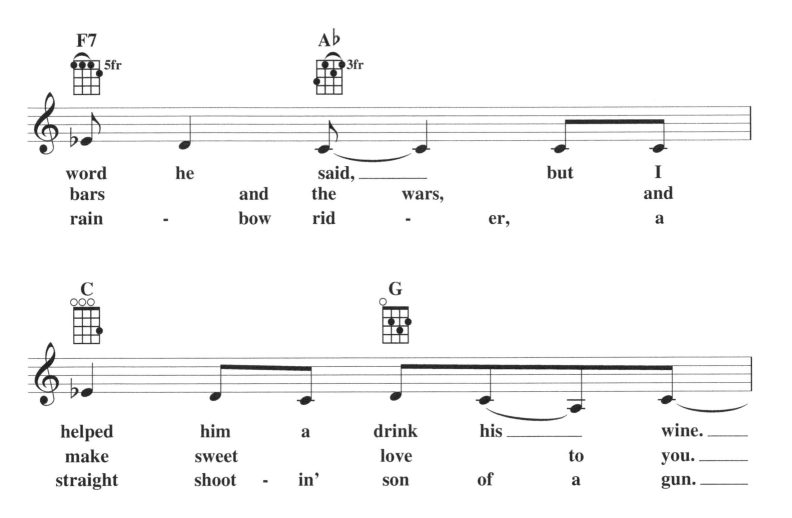

word	he		said, _____		but	I
bars	and		the	wars,		and
rain	-	bow	rid	-	er,	a

helped	him	a	drink	his _____		wine. _____
make	sweet		love		to	you. _____
straight	shoot	- in'	son	of	a	gun. _____

_____	And	he	al - ways	had	some	might - y	fine
_____	Yes,	I'd	make	sweet		love	to
_____	I said,	a	straight	shoot - in'	son	of	a

Chorus

wine. }			
you. }	Sing - ing	joy	to the	world,
gun. }			

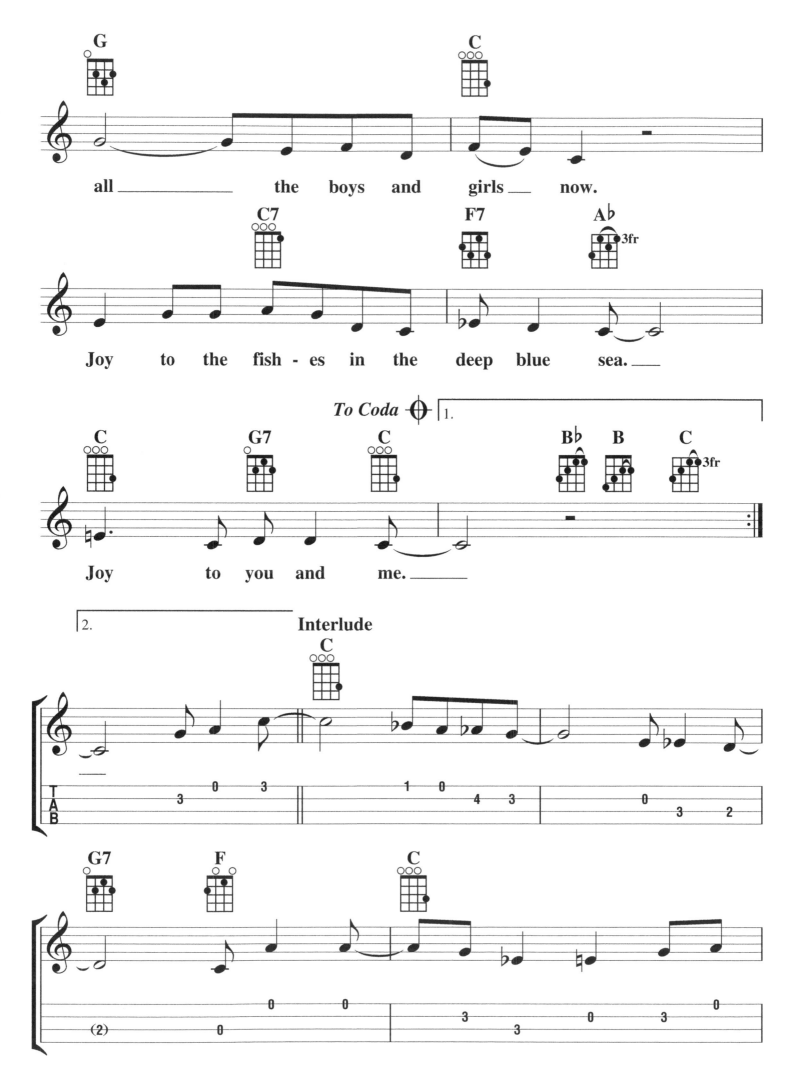

all _____ the boys and girls __ now.

Joy to the fish - es in the deep blue sea. __

To Coda ⊕

1.

Joy to you and me. _____

2.

Interlude

G7 **F** **C**

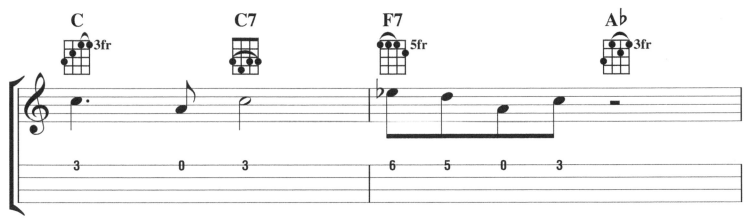

D.S. al Coda

Coda

Bridge

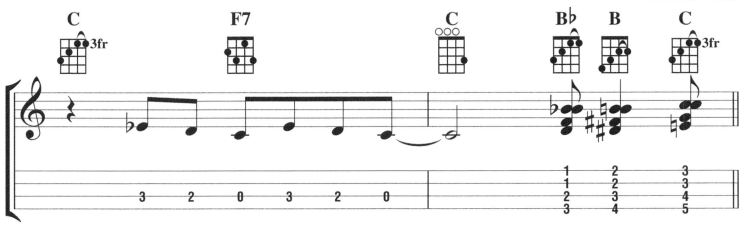

Joy _____ to _____

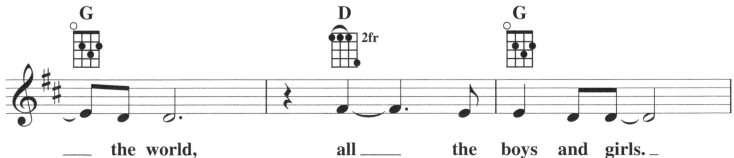

_____ the world, all _____ the boys and girls. _

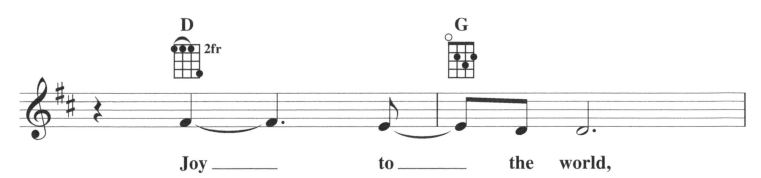

Joy _____ to _____ the world,

joy _____ to you and me.

Outro-Chorus

Joy   to   the   world,

all _____ the boys and girls.

Joy   to   the   fish - es   in   the   deep blue   sea. ___

Repeat & fade

Joy   to   you   and   me. _____

Light My Fire

Words and Music by The Doors

First note

Intro

Moderately

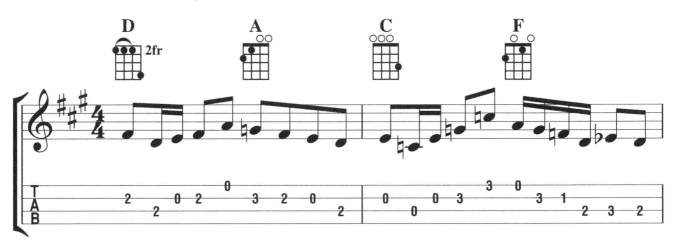

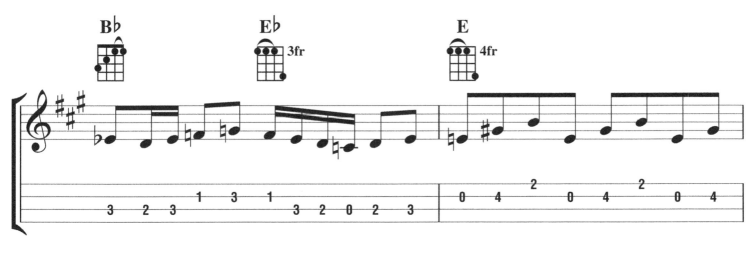

Verse

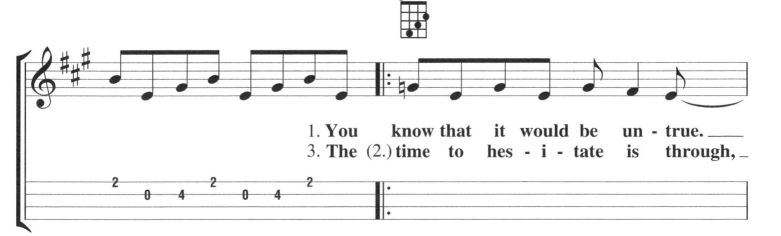

1. You know that it would be un - true. ____
3. The (2.) time to hes - i - tate is through, ____

You know that I would be a li - ar,
no time to wal - low in the mire. _____

if I was to say to you, _____
Try now, we can on - ly lose, _____ and our

"Girl, we could - n't get much high - er."
love be - come a fu - n'ral pyre. _____

Chorus

Come on, ba - by, light my fire. ___
Come on, ba - by, light my fire. _

To Coda ⊕ | 1.

Try to set the night on fire. ___ 2. The

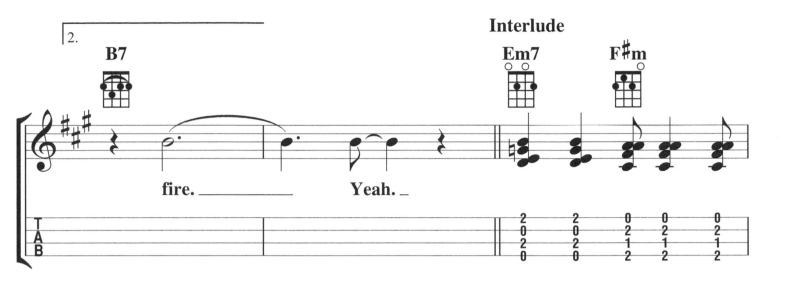

Interlude

fire. _____ Yeah. _

D.C. al Coda

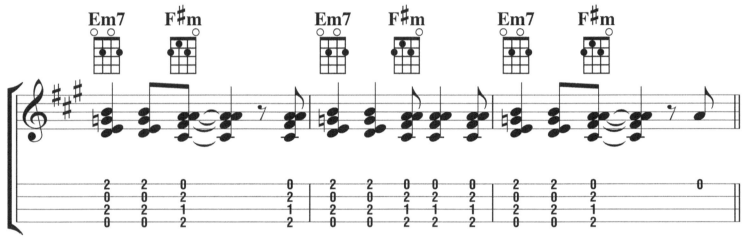

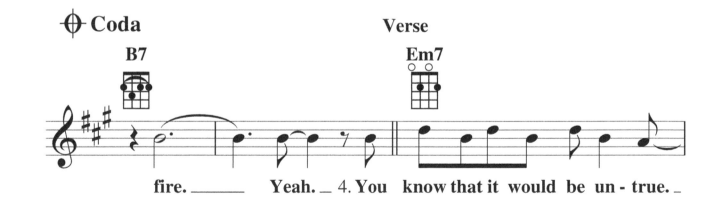

Coda

Verse

fire. _____ Yeah. _ 4. You know that it would be un - true. _

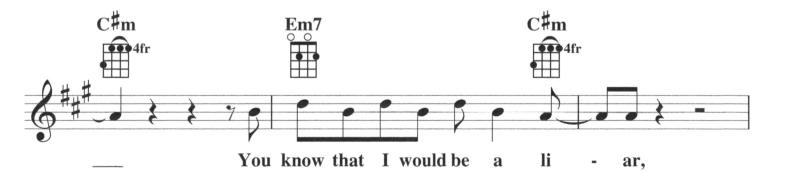

___ You know that I would be a li - ar,

Try to set the night on   fire. _____

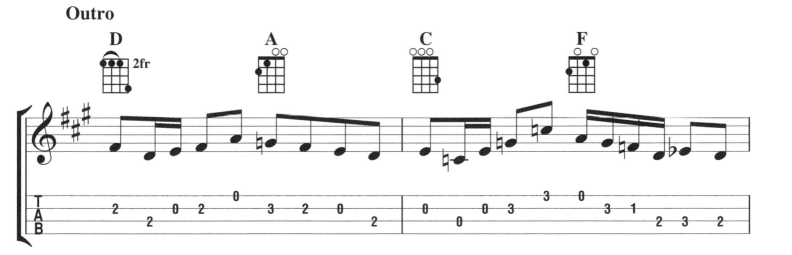

Try   to   set   the night on   fire! _____

Outro

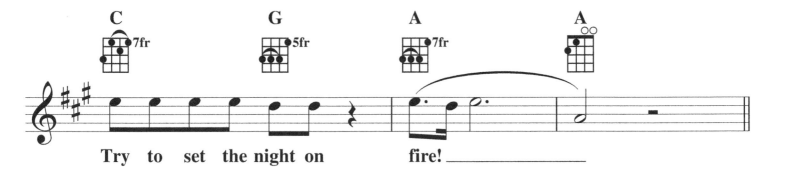

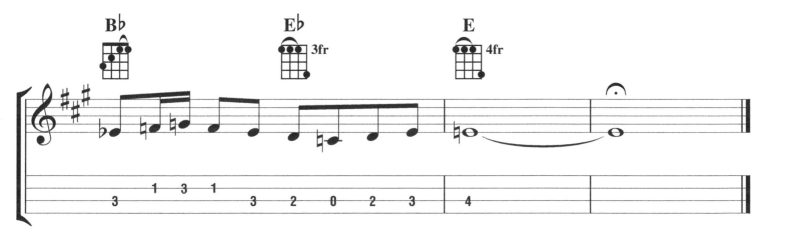

Leaving on a Jet Plane

Words and Music by John Denver

First note
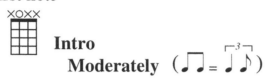

Intro
Moderately

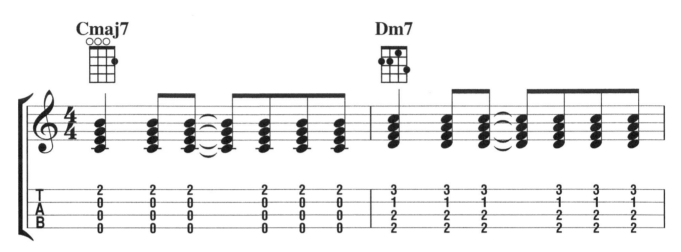

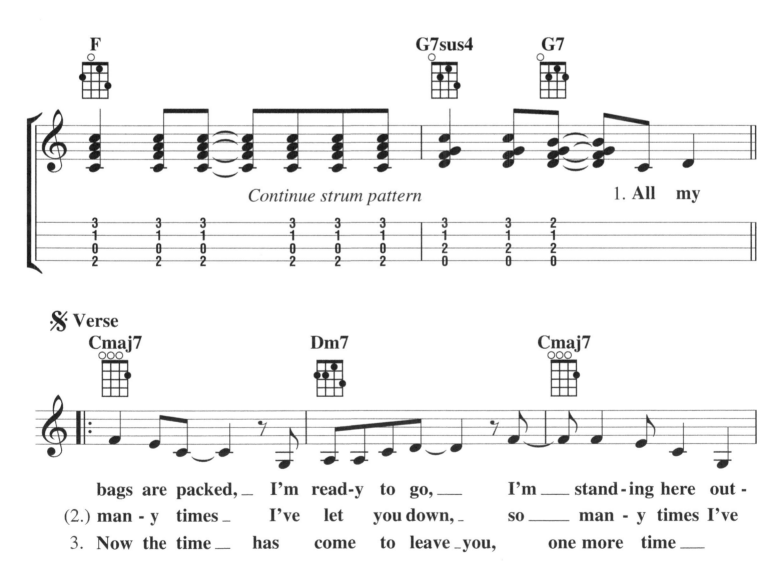

Continue strum pattern

1. All my

%. **Verse**

bags are packed, _ I'm read-y to go, _ I'm ___ stand-ing here out-

(2.) man - y times _ I've let you down, _ so ____ man - y times I've

3. Now the time _ has come to leave _ you, one more time ___

Dm7   Cmaj7   F

side your door, __   I hate to wake __ you   up   to   say   good -
played a - round;   I tell you now __   they don't mean   a
let me kiss you,   then close your eyes __   I'll   be   on   my

G   G7   Cmaj7

bye. _____   But the dawn __ is break - in', it's
thing. _____   Ev - 'ry place __ I go I
way. _____   Dream __ a - bout the

Dm7   Cmaj7

ear - ly morn', __   tax - i's wait - in' he's
think of you, __   ev - 'ry song I sing I
days to come __   when I won't have to

Dm7   Cmaj7

blow - in' his horn, __   al - read - y I'm so
sing for you, __   when I come back I'll
leave a - lone, __   a - bout the times

Dm   G   G7

              ⌐— 3 —⌐

lone - some I could cry. _____   So ⎞
wear your wed - ding ring. _____   So ⎬
I won't have to say: _____   ⎠

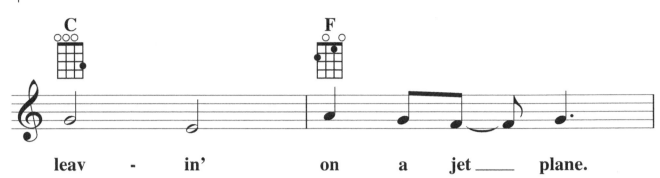

⊕ Coda

leav - in' on a jet ___ plane.

I don't know when I'll be back ___ a - gain.

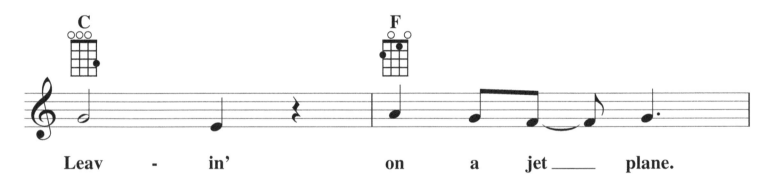

Leav - in' on a jet ___ plane.

I don't know when I'll be back ___ a-gain. Oh,

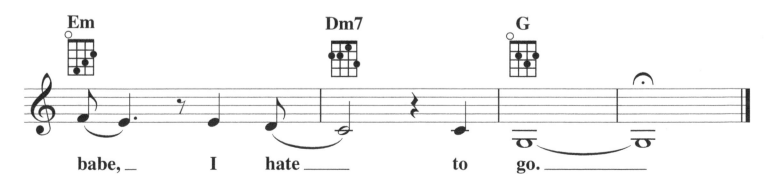

babe, ___ I hate ___ to go. ___

Love Grows
(Where My Rosemary Goes)

Words and Music by Tony Macaulay and Barry Mason

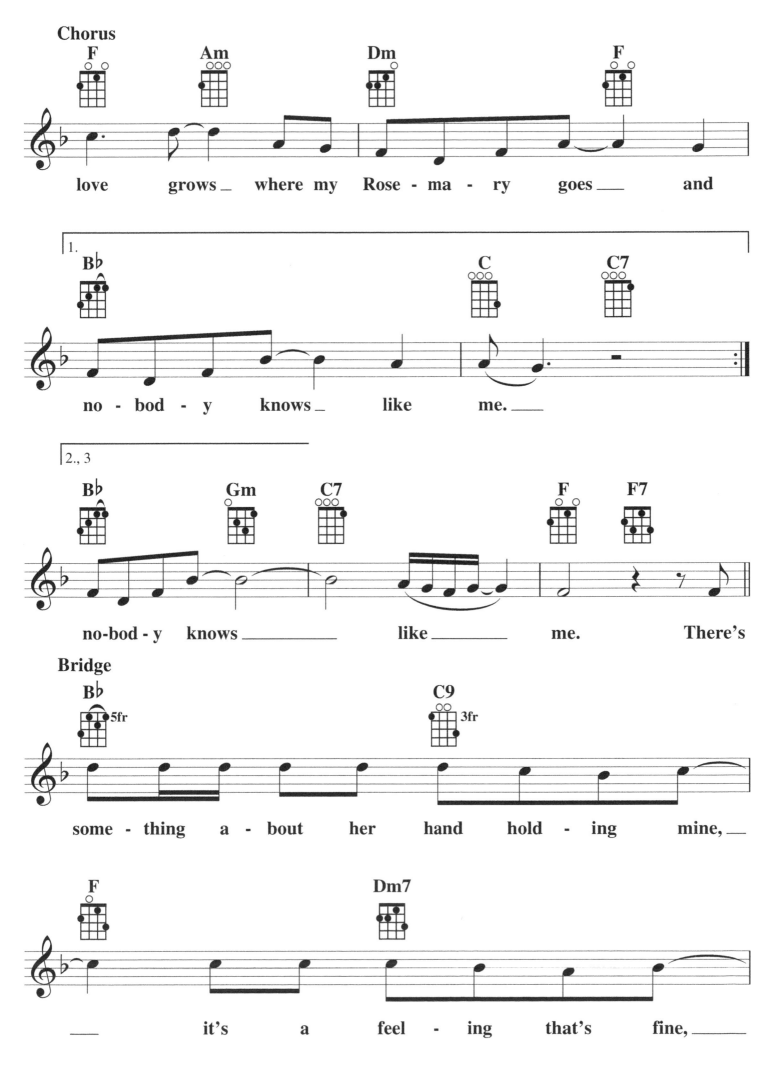

Chorus

F   Am   Dm   F

love   grows &_   where my Rose - ma - ry   goes ___   and

1.

Bb   C   C7

no - bod - y   knows __   like   me. ___

2., 3

Bb   Gm   C7   F   F7

no-bod - y   knows _____   like _____ me.   There's

Bridge

Bb   C9

some - thing a - bout   her   hand   hold - ing   mine, ___

F   Dm7

___   it's   a   feel - ing   that's   fine, _____

and I've just got to say, ____ "Hey." _ She's

real - ly got a mag - i - cal spell ____

To Coda ⊕

____ and it's work-ing so well ____ that I can't get a - way. _

⊕ **Coda**

D.S. al Coda

3. I'm

4. I'm _

Verse

____ a luck - y fel - la and I ____

66

just got - ta tell her that ____

___ I love her end - less - ly. ____

Outro-Chorus

_____ Be - cause love grows _ where my

Rose - ma - ry goes _ and no - bod - y knows ____

___ like _____ me. _____

Mellow Yellow

Words and Music by Donovan Leitch

Chorus

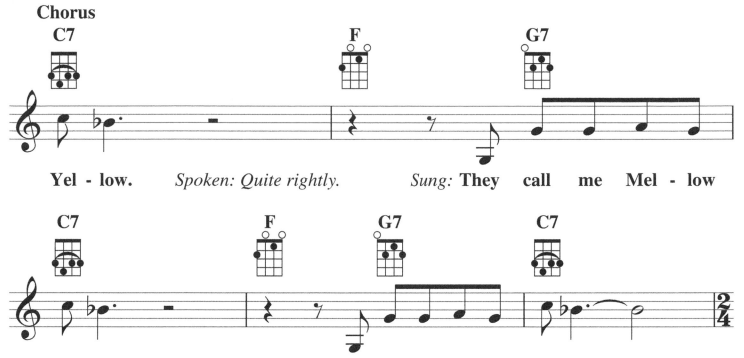

Yel - low.   *Spoken: Quite rightly.*   *Sung:* **They   call   me   Mel - low**

Yel-low. *Spoken: Quite rightly. Sung:* **They call me Mel - low   Yel-low.** ____

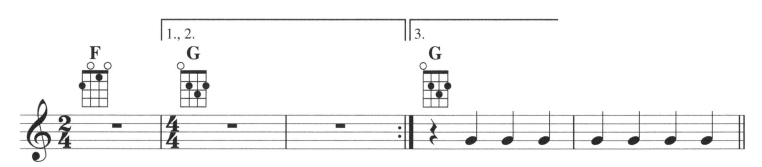

So mel-low, he's so mel-low.

Interlude

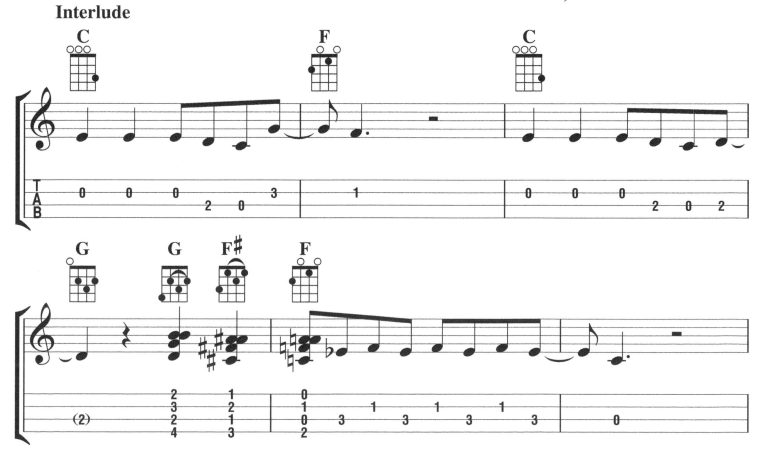

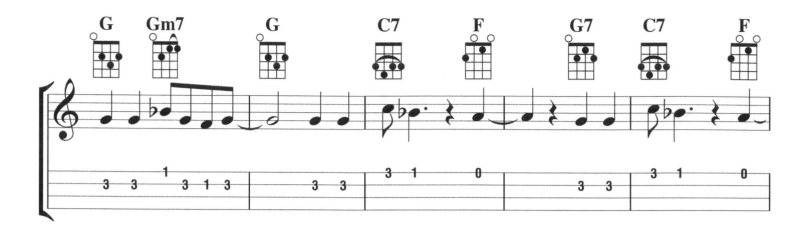

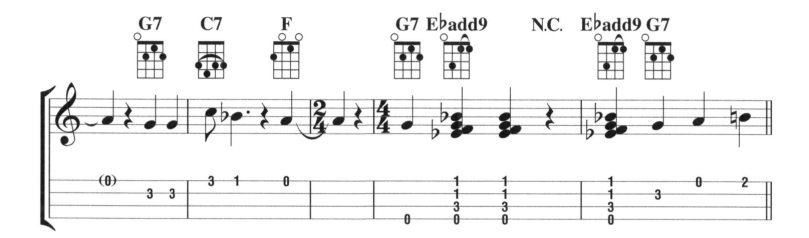

 Verse

4. E - lec - tri - cal ba - nan - a.   is   gon-na be a sud-den ___ craze. ___
5. Saf - fron.   Yeah. ___   I'm   just   mad a-bout her. ___

___   E - lec - tri - cal ba - nan - a ___   is
___   I'm ah, just mad a-bout ah, Saf - fron, ___

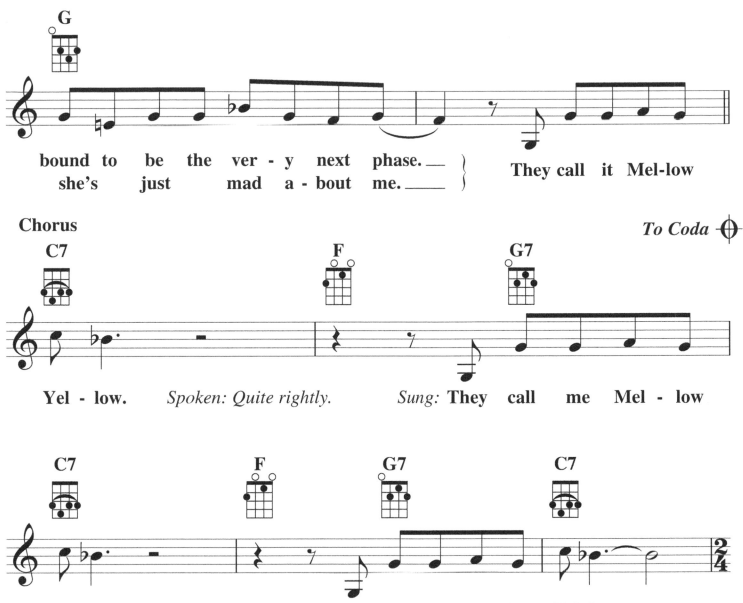

bound to be the ver - y next phase. ____
she's just mad a - bout me. ____

They call it Mel-low

Chorus

To Coda ⊕

C7   **F**   **G7**

Yel - low.   *Spoken: Quite rightly.*   *Sung:* They call me Mel - low

C7   **F**   **G7**   **C7**

Yel - low. *Spoken: Quite rightly. Sung:* They call me Mel - low Yel - low. ____

D.S. al Coda

F   **G**

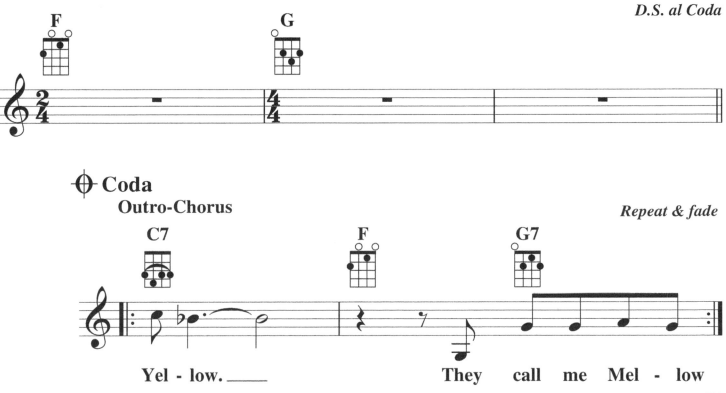

⊕ **Coda**
Outro-Chorus

Repeat & fade

C7   **F**   **G7**

Yel - low. ____   They call me Mel - low

Mr. Tambourine Man

Words and Music by Bob Dylan

go-in' to. ___   Hey,   Mis-ter Tam - bou-rine _ Man, _

play a   song _   for _ me. ___   In the   jin - gle _ jan - gle

morn-in',   I'll come _ fol - low-in'   you.

Verse

Take me for ___ a   trip up - on ___ your _ mag-ic ___ swirl-ing _ ship. _

___   All my   sens - es _ have _ been _ stripped,   and my hands _

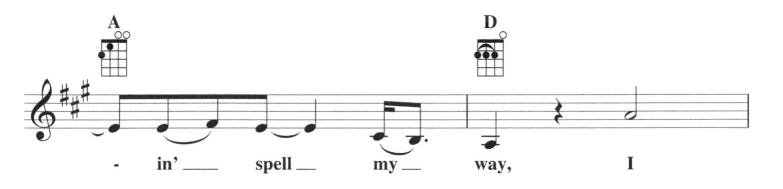

- in' ____ spell ____ my ____ way,   I

D.S. al Coda

prom-ise to ____ go un - der it. ____

⊕ Coda

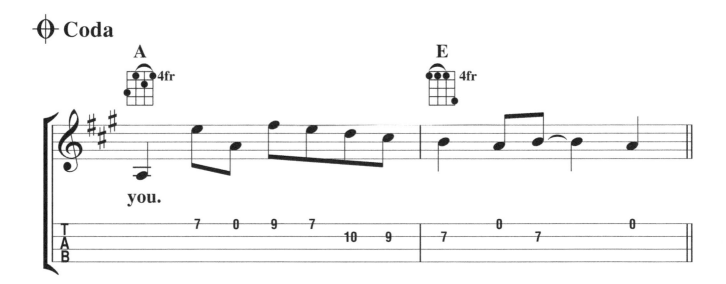

you.

Outro

Repeat & fade

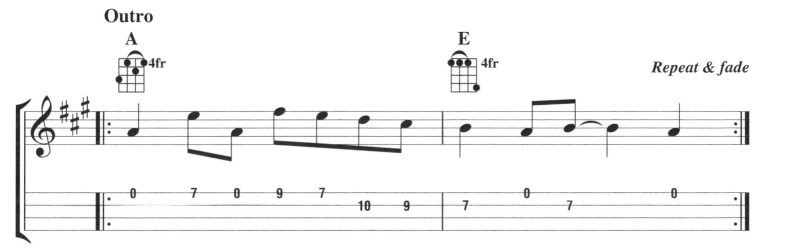

Monday, Monday

Words and Music by John Phillips

First note

Intro
Moderately

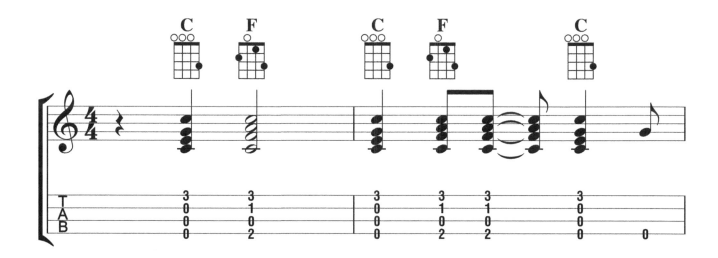

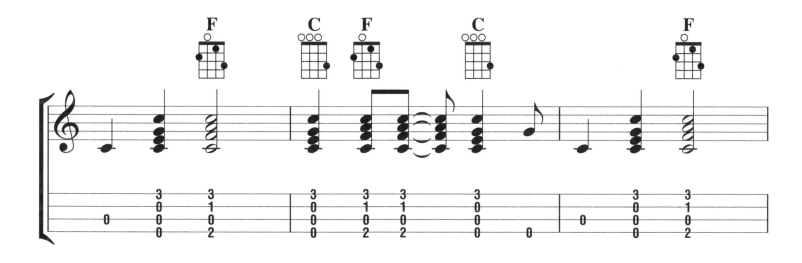

𝄋 Verse

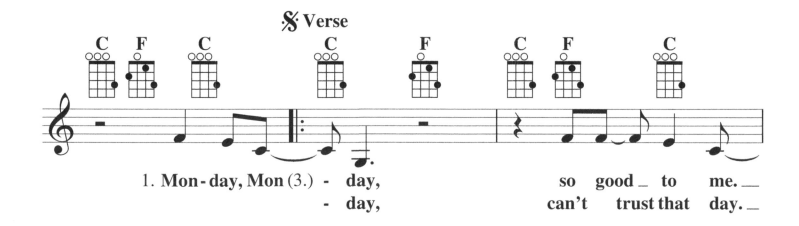

1. **Mon-day, Mon** (3.) **- day,**   so good ___ to   me. ___
                      - day,   can't   trust that   day. ___

Mon - day morn - in',   it was   all __
Mon - day, Mon - day,   some - times it

__ I hoped __ it would   be. _____   Oh, Mon - day
just turns   out that   way. _____   Oh, Mon - day

morn - in',   Mon - day morn - in' could - n't guar - an - tee, __
morn - in', you gave me no warn - in'   of what was to be, __

that Mon - day eve - nin' you would still __   be here _ with me. __
oh, Mon - day, Mon - day how could you leave __   and not   take me? _

__
__   2. Mon - day, Mon -

Ev-'ry oth-er day, ____ ev-'ry oth-er day, ev-'ry oth-er day of the week is fine, yeah! ____

But when-ev-er Mon-day comes, but when-ev-er Mon-day comes you can find me cry-in' all of the time. ____ 3. Mon-day, Mon-

cry-in' all of the time. _____

Mon-day, Mon-

Outro

- day, can't _ trust that day.

Mon - day, Mon - day, it just turns out that

way. _ Mon - day, Mon - day,

won't go a - way. __ Mon - day, Mon -

- day, it's here _ to stay. _____

Morning Has Broken

Musical Arrangement by Cat Stevens
Words by Eleanor Farjeon

1., 4. Morn - ing has bro - ken like the first _
2. Sweet the rain's new fall, sun - lit from

morn - ing.
heav - en.

Black-bird has spo - ken
Like the first dew fall

like the first bird.
on the first grass.

Praise for the
Praise for the

sing - ing,
sweet - ness

praise for the morn - ing,
of the wet gar - den,

praise   for   them   spring - ing
sprung   in   com   -   plete   -   ness

Interlude

fresh   from ___ the   world.
where   his feet   pass.

3. Mine is the sun - light, mine is the morn - ing.
Born of the one light E - den saw
play. Praise with e - la - tion, praise ev - 'ry

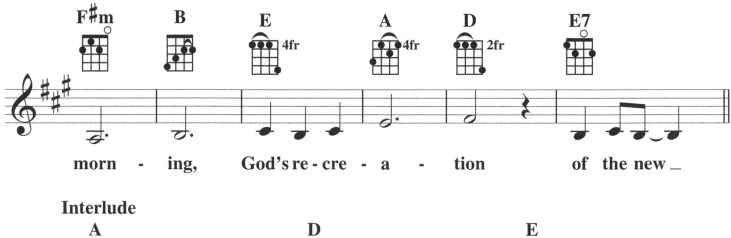

morn - ing, God's re - cre - a - tion of the new ___

Interlude

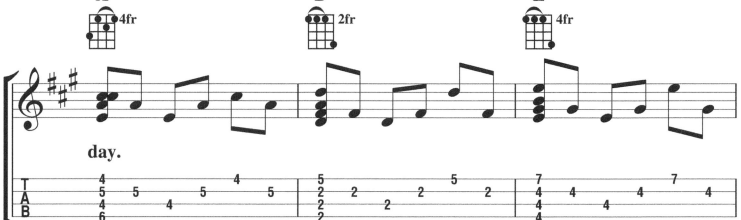

day.

D.C. al Fine
(take 2nd ending)

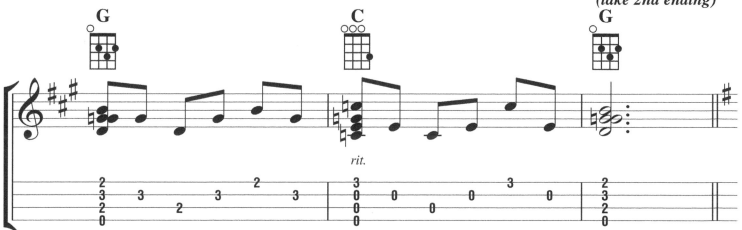

rit.

83

New World Coming

Words and Music by Barry Mann and Cynthia Weil

One Toke Over the Line

Words and Music by Michael Brewer and Thomas E. Shipley

home, sweet Mar - y, hop - in' that the train is on time. _

To Coda ⊕

Sit - tin' down - town in a rail - way sta - tion, one toke o - ver the line. _

Verse

1. Who _____ do you love? _____
2. I _____ sailed a - way _____

___ I hope it's me. ____ I've been
___ a coun - try mile ____ and now I'm re -

chang - in', as you can plain - ly see. ____
turn - in', and show - in' off my smile. _ I

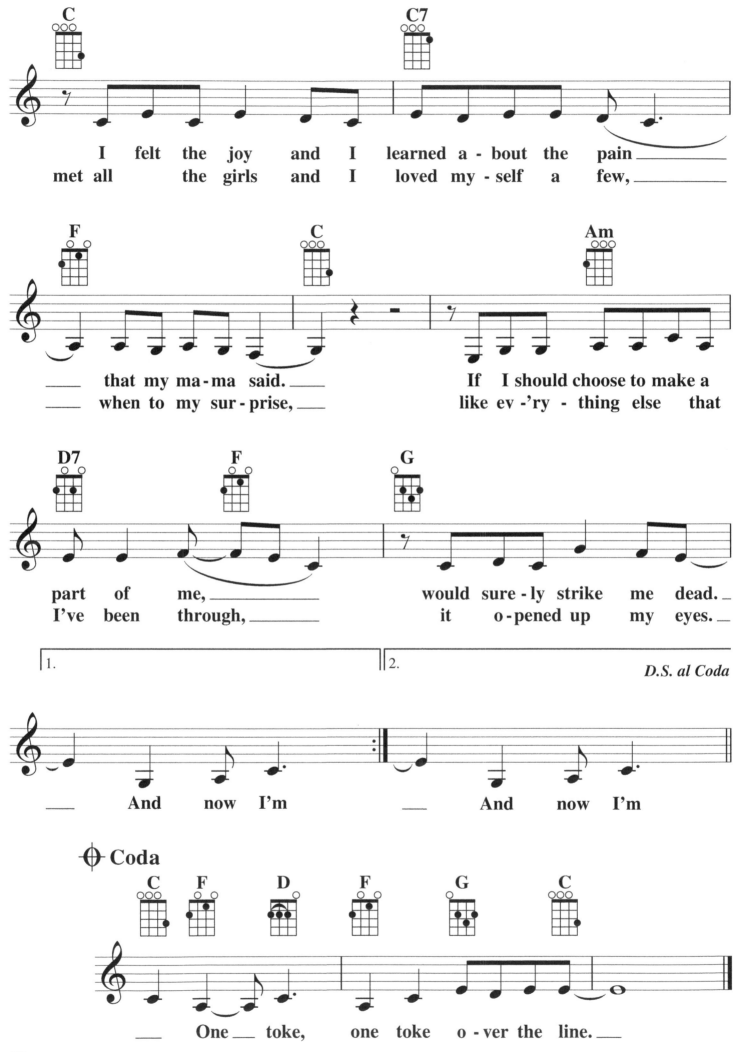

I felt the joy and I learned a - bout the pain _____
met all the girls and I loved my - self a few, _____

_____ that my ma - ma said. _____
_____ when to my sur - prise, _____

If I should choose to make a
like ev -'ry - thing else that

part of me, _____
I've been through, _____

would sure - ly strike me dead. _
it o -pened up my eyes. _

1.
2.

D.S. al Coda

_ And now I'm
_ And now I'm

Coda

C   F   D   F   G   C

One _ toke, one toke o - ver the line. _

88

San Francisco
(Be Sure to Wear Some Flowers in Your Hair)
Words and Music by John Phillips

Time in a Bottle

Words and Music by Jim Croce

Am6 Dm6 Dm Dsus2

the first thing ___ that I'd like to do
if words could ___ make wish - es come true,
and dreams that had nev - er come true.

E7 Am Am7 F

is to save ev -'ry day 'til e - ter - ni - ty ___
I'd save ev -'ry day like a treas - ure and
The box would be emp - ty ex - cept for the

Dm Am Dm7

pass - es a - way just to spend them with
then a - gain I would spend them with
mem - 'ry of how they were an - swered by

1. 2.

E7

you.   2. If   But there
you.
you.

Bridge

A Amaj7 A6

nev - er seems _ to be e-nough time _ to do the things _ you

want to do once you find them. _____

I've looked a-round e-nough ____ to know ____ that

you're the one I want to go through time with.

To Coda ⊕

D.C. al Coda
(take 2nd ending)

⊕ **Coda**

Outro

Play 3 times

What the World Needs Now Is Love

Lyric by Hal David
Music by Burt Bacharach

To Coda ⊕

C6

B7

No, not just for some, _____ but for ev - 'ry - one. _____

Verse

Em9

_____

1. Lord, we don't need an - oth - er
2. Lord, we don't need an - oth - er

Em7

Dm7

moun - tain, there ___ are moun - tains ___ and
mead - ow, there ___ are corn fields ___ and

G7

Cmaj7

3

hill - sides _____ e - nough to climb. ___
wheat fields _____ e - nough to grow. ___

C6

Dm7

There _____ are o - ceans _____ and
There _____ are sun - beams _____ and

Turn! Turn! Turn!
(To Everything There Is a Season)

Words from the Book of Ecclesiastes
Adaptation and Music by Pete Seeger

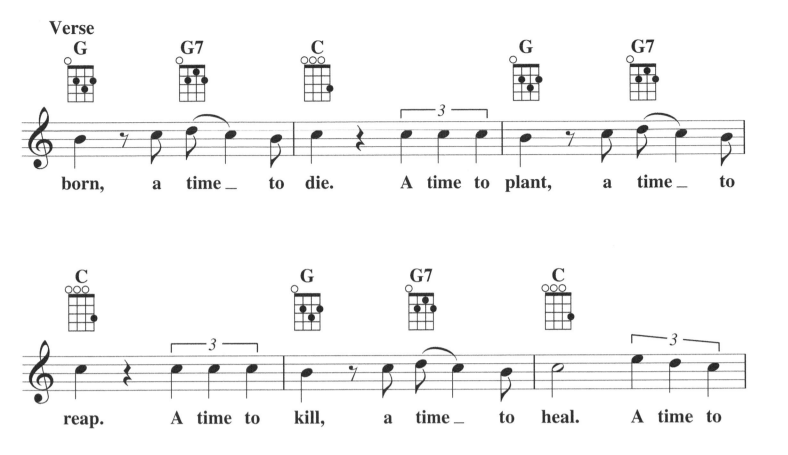

Verse

born, a time ___ to die. A time to plant, a time ___ to

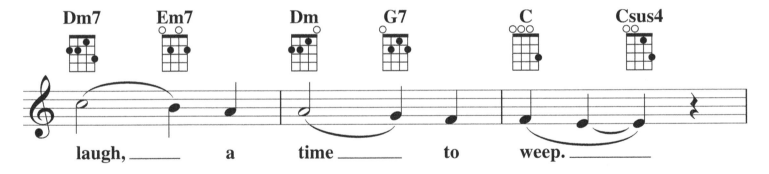

reap. A time to kill, a time ___ to heal. A time to

To Coda ⊕

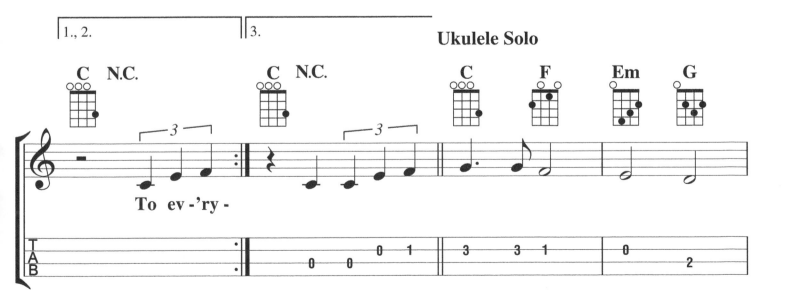

laugh, _____ a time _____ to weep. _____

Ukulele Solo

To ev - 'ry -

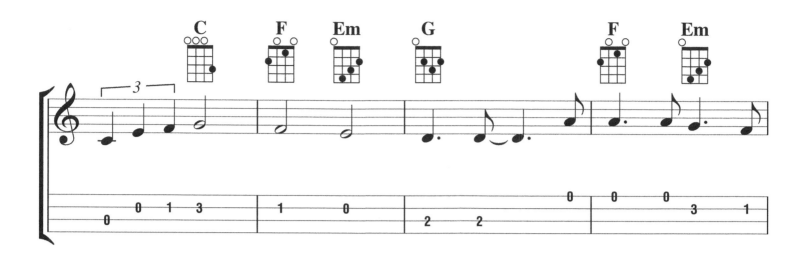

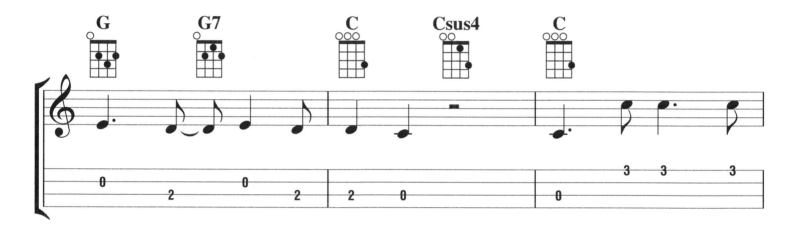

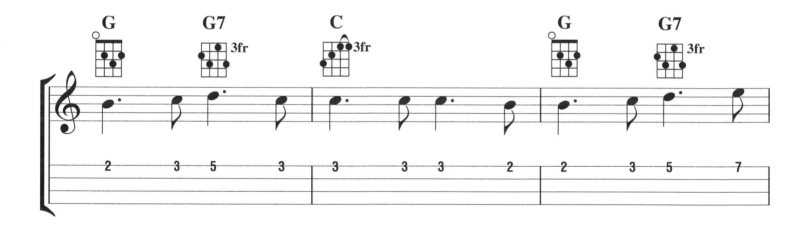

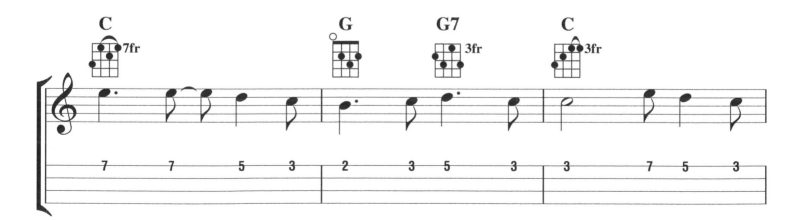

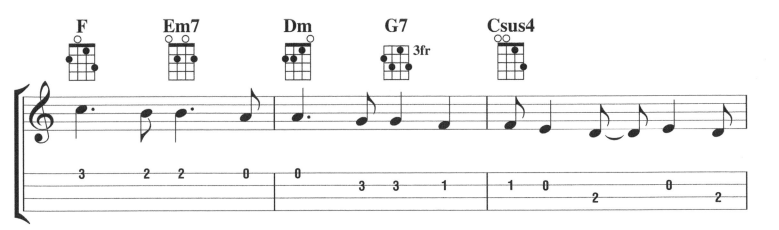

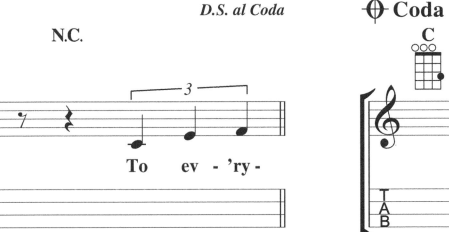

D.S. al Coda   ⊕ *Coda*

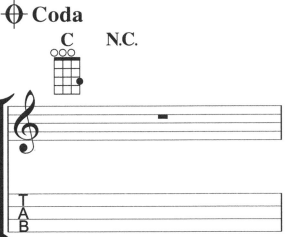

To ev - 'ry -

Outro   *Repeat & fade*

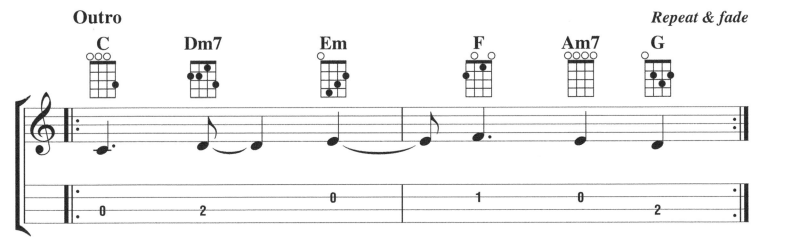

Additional Lyrics

2. A time to build up, a time to break down;
   A time to dance, a time to mourn;
   A time to cast away stones,
   A time to gather stones together.

3. A time of love, a time of hate;
   A time of war, a time of peace;
   A time you may embrace,
   A time to refrain from embracing.

4. A time to gain, a time to lose;
   A time to rend, a time to sew;
   A time for love, a time for hate;
   A time for peace, I swear it's not too late.

We Shall Overcome

Musical and Lyrical Adaptation by Zilphia Horton, Frank Hamilton, Guy Carawan and Pete Seeger
Inspired by African American Gospel Singing, members of the Food and Tobacco Workers Union
Charleston, SC, and the southern Civil Rights Movement

1. We shall o - ver - come, _____
2. We'll walk hand in hand, _____
3.–6. *See additional lyrics*

we shall o - ver - come, _____
we'll walk hand in hand, _____

we shall o - ver -
we'll walk hand in

come some day. _____ } Oh, ____
hand some day. _____

Chorus

deep in my heart I do be - lieve, we shall o - ver-

1.– 5. | 6.

come some day. _____

Additional Lyrics

3. We shall live in peace,
   We shall live in peace,
   We shall live in peace some day.

4. We shall all be free,
   We shall all be free,
   We shall all be free some day.

5. We are not afraid,
   We are not afraid,
   We are not afraid today.

6. *Repeat Verse 1*

White Rabbit

Words and Music by Grace Slick

First note

A Whiter Shade of Pale

Words and Music by Keith Reid, Gary Brooker and Matthew Fisher

1. We skipped the light fan-dan-go, _____
2. She said, "There is _____ no rea-son, _____

When we called out for an - oth - er drink _____
And al - though my eyes were o - pen _____

the wait - er brought _ a tray. _
they might just as well _ been closed. _

And so it

Chorus

was _____ that lat - er _____ as the mill - er told his

tale, _ that her face, at first just ghost-ly, turned a

1.
whit - er _____ shade of pale. _____

2.
pale. _____

UKULELE NOTATION LEGEND

THE MUSICAL STAFF shows pitches and rhythms and is divided by bar lines into measures. Pitches are named after the first seven letters of the alphabet.

TABLATURE graphically represents the ukulele fingerboard. Each horizontal line represents a a string, and each number represents a fret.

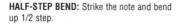
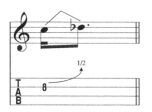

2nd string, 3rd fret — 1st & 2nd strings open, played together — open F chord

HALF-STEP BEND: Strike the note and bend up 1/2 step.

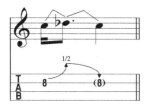

WHOLE-STEP BEND: Strike the note and bend up one step.

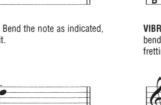

GRACE NOTE BEND: Strike the note and immediately bend up as indicated.

SLIGHT (MICROTONE) BEND: Strike the note and bend up 1/4 step.

BEND AND RELEASE: Strike the note and bend up as indicated, then release back to the original note. Only the first note is struck.

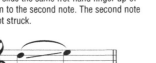

PRE-BEND: Bend the note as indicated, then strike it.

VIBRATO: The string is vibrated by rapidly bending and releasing the note with the fretting hand.

HAMMER-ON: Strike the first (lower) note with one finger, then sound the higher note (on the same string) with another finger by fretting it without picking.

PULL-OFF: Place both fingers on the notes to be sounded. Strike the first note and without picking, pull the finger off to sound the second (lower) note.

LEGATO SLIDE: Strike the first note and then slide the same fret-hand finger up or down to the second note. The second note is not struck.

SHIFT SLIDE: Same as legato slide, except the second note is struck.

TRILL: Very rapidly alternate between the notes indicated by continuously hammering on and pulling off.

TREMOLO PICKING: The note is picked as rapidly and continuously as possible.

NOTE: Tablature numbers in parentheses mean:

1. The note is being sustained over a system (note in standard notation is tied), or

2. The note is sustained, but a new articulation (such as a hammer-on, pull-off, slide or vibrato) begins, or

3. The note is a barely audible "ghost" note (note in standard notation is also in parentheses).

Additional Musical Definitions

>	*(accent)*	• Accentuate note (play it louder)
•	*(staccato)*	• Play the note short
D.S. al Coda		• Go back to the sign (𝄋), then play until the measure marked "*To Coda*," then skip to the section labelled "**Coda**."
D.C. al Fine		• Go back to the beginning of the song and play until the measure marked "*Fine*" (end).
N.C.		• No chord.
		• Repeat measures between signs.
1. 2.		• When a repeated section has different endings, play the first ending only the first time and the second ending only the second time.

The Best Collections for Ukulele

The Best Songs Ever
70 songs have now been arranged for ukulele. Includes: Always • Bohemian Rhapsody • Memory • My Favorite Things • Over the Rainbow • Piano Man • What a Wonderful World • Yesterday • You Raise Me Up • and more.
00282413........$17.99

Campfire Songs for Ukulele
30 favorites to sing as you roast marshmallows and strum your uke around the campfire. Includes: God Bless the U.S.A. • Hallelujah • The House of the Rising Sun • I Walk the Line • Puff the Magic Dragon • Wagon Wheel • You Are My Sunshine • and more.
00129170 ....$15.99

The Daily Ukulele
arr. Liz and Jim Beloff
Strum a different song everyday with easy arrangements of 365 of your favorite songs in one big songbook! Includes favorites by the Beatles, Beach Boys, and Bob Dylan, folk songs, pop songs, kids' songs, Christmas carols, and Broadway and Hollywood tunes, all with a spiral binding for ease of use.
00240356 Original Edition.................$44.99
00240681 Leap Year Edition $44.99
00119270 Portable Edition $39.99

Disney Hits for Ukulele
Play 23 of your favorite Disney songs on your ukulele. Includes: The Bare Necessities • Cruella De Vil • Do You Want to Build a Snowman? • Kiss the Girl • Lava • Let It Go • Once upon a Dream • A Whole New World • and more.
00151250 ....$16.99

Also available:
00291547 Disney Fun Songs for Ukulele $17.99
00701708 Disney Songs for Ukulele..........$15.99
00334696 First 50 Disney Songs on Ukulele.....$22.99

First 50 Songs You Should Play on Ukulele
An amazing collec-tion of 50 accessible, must-know favorites: Edelweiss • Hey, Soul Sister • I Walk the Line • I'm Yours • Imagine • Over the Rainbow • Peaceful Easy Feeling • The Rainbow Connection • Riptide • more.
00149250 ....$19.99

Also available:
00292982 First 50 Melodies on Ukulele.......$16.99
00289029 First 50 Songs on Solo Ukulele $16.99
00347437 First 50 Songs to Strum on Uke.....$19.99

40 Most Streamed Songs for Ukulele
40 top hits that sound great on uke! Includes: Despacito • Feel It Still • Girls like You • Happier • Havana • High Hopes • The Middle • Perfect • 7 Rings • Shallow • Shape of You • Something Just like This • Stay • Sucker • Sunflower • Sweet but Psycho • Thank U, Next • There's Nothing Holdin' Me Back • Without Me • and more!
00298113 ....$17.99

The 4 Chord Songbook
With just 4 chords, you can play 50 hot songs on your ukulele! Songs include: Brown Eyed Girl • Do Wah Diddy Diddy • Hey Ya! • Ho Hey • Jessie's Girl • Let It Be • One Love • Stand by Me • Toes • With or Without You • and many more.
00142050........$17.99

Also available:
00141143 The 3-Chord Songbook...........$17.99

Pop Songs for Kids
30 easy pop favorites for kids to play on uke, including: Brave • Can't Stop the Feeling! • Feel It Still • Fight Song • Happy • Havana • House of Gold • How Far I'll Go • Let It Go • Remember Me (Ernesto de la Cruz) • Rewrite the Stars • Roar • Shake It Off • Story of My Life • What Makes You Beautiful • and more.
00284415 ....$17.99

Simple Songs for Ukulele
50 favorites for standard G-C-E-A ukulele tuning, including: All Along the Watchtower • Can't Help Falling in Love • Don't Worry, Be Happy • Ho Hey • I'm Yours • King of the Road • Sweet Home Alabama • You Are My Sunshine • and more.
00156815........$15.99

Also available:
00276644 More Simple Songs for Ukulele.....$14.99

Top Hits of 2022
This collection features 16 of today's top hits arranged with vocal melody, lyrics, and chord diagrams for standard G-C-E-A tuning for ukulele. Songs include: As It Was • Bam Bam • Carolina • Enemy • Freedom • Glimpse of Us • Hold My Hand • Light Switch • Love Me More • Nobody like U • Numb Little Bug • On My Way • Running up That Hill • and more.
01100312.............................$14.99

Also available:
00355553 Top Hits of 2020.................$14.99
00302274 Top Hits of 2019.................$14.99

Ukulele: The Most Requested Songs
Strum & Sing Series
Cherry Lane Music
Nearly 50 favorites all expertly arranged for ukulele! Includes: Bubbly • Build Me Up, Buttercup • Cecilia • Georgia on My Mind • Kokomo • L-O-V-E • Your Body Is a Wonderland • and more.
02501453.............................$15.99

The Ultimate Ukulele Fake Book
Uke enthusiasts will love this giant, spiral-bound collection of over 400 songs for uke! Includes: Crazy • Dancing Queen • Downtown • Fields of Gold • Happy • Hey Jude • 7 Years • Summertime • Thinking Out Loud • Thriller • Wagon Wheel • and more.
00175500 9" x 12" Edition $45.00
00319997 5.5" x 8.5" Edition $39.99

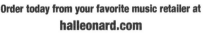

UKULELE

1. POP HITS
00701451 Book/CD Pack $15.99

3. HAWAIIAN FAVORITES
00701453 Book/Online Audio $14.99

4. CHILDREN'S SONGS
00701454 Book/Online Audio $14.99

5. CHRISTMAS SONGS
00701696 Book/CD Pack $12.99

6. LENNON & McCARTNEY
00701723 Book/Online Audio $12.99

7. DISNEY FAVORITES
00701724 Book/Online Audio $14.99

8. CHART HITS
00701745 Book/CD Pack $15.99

9. THE SOUND OF MUSIC
00701784 Book/CD Pack $14.99

10. MOTOWN
00701964 Book/CD Pack $12.99

11. CHRISTMAS STRUMMING
00702458 Book/Online Audio $12.99

12. BLUEGRASS FAVORITES
00702584 Book/CD Pack $12.99

13. UKULELE SONGS
00702599 Book/CD Pack $12.99

14. JOHNNY CASH
00702615 Book/Online Audio $15.99

15. COUNTRY CLASSICS
00702834 Book/CD Pack $12.99

16. STANDARDS
00702835 Book/CD Pack $12.99

17. POP STANDARDS
00702836 Book/CD Pack $12.99

18. IRISH SONGS
00703086 Book/Online Audio $12.99

19. BLUES STANDARDS
00703087 Book/CD Pack $12.99

20. FOLK POP ROCK
00703088 Book/CD Pack $12.99

21. HAWAIIAN CLASSICS
00703097 Book/CD Pack $12.99

22. ISLAND SONGS
00703098 Book/CD Pack $12.99

23. TAYLOR SWIFT
00221966 Book/Online Audio $16.99

24. WINTER WONDERLAND
00101871 Book/CD Pack $12.99

25. GREEN DAY
00110398 Book/CD Pack $14.99

26. BOB MARLEY
00110399 Book/Online Audio $14.99

27. TIN PAN ALLEY
00116358 Book/CD Pack $12.99

28. STEVIE WONDER
00116736 Book/CD Pack $14.99

29. OVER THE RAINBOW & OTHER FAVORITES
00117076 Book/Online Audio $15.99

30. ACOUSTIC SONGS
00122336 Book/CD Pack $14.99

31. JASON MRAZ
00124166 Book/CD Pack $14.99

32. TOP DOWNLOADS
00127507 Book/CD Pack $14.99

33. CLASSICAL THEMES
00127892 Book/Online Audio $14.99

34. CHRISTMAS HITS
00128602 Book/CD Pack $14.99

35. SONGS FOR BEGINNERS
00129009 Book/Online Audio $14.99

36. ELVIS PRESLEY HAWAII
00138199 Book/Online Audio $14.99

37. LATIN
00141191 Book/Online Audio $14.99

38. JAZZ
00141192 Book/Online Audio $14.99

39. GYPSY JAZZ
00146559 Book/Online Audio $15.99

40. TODAY'S HITS
00160845 Book/Online Audio $14.99

HAL•LEONARD®

www.halleonard.com

Prices, contents, and availability subject to change without notice.